From Rags to Riches
A Story of Abu Dhabi

Student Edition

By
Mohammed Al Fahim

Retold by
Patrick Dougherty

Edited by
Melanie Gobert

Printing authorization:
Approval of National Media Council, Abu Dhabi
Number : 1/100122/29917
Year : 2011

ISBN : 978 9948 16 3305

Published by Makarem LLC
P O Box 7555, Abu Dhabi, United Arab Emirates
email: makarem1@emirates.net.ae
website: www.makarem.ae

Printed in Dubai

To **Sheikh Zayed bin Sultan Al Nahyan**;
to my father, **Abduljalil Al Fahim**,
and to all the children of the
United Arab Emirates.

Contents

Foreword

I was very happy to learn Dr Melanie Gobert has chosen my book Rags to Riches – The Story of Abu Dhabi for her research project at the Higher Colleges of Technology.

It was with all my best wishes and whole hearted willingness gave her my consent for the same. I was told that the aim of her project was to re work the contents of the book in a more simplified manner to make it easier for the school and college students to comprehend, understand and to make use of its historical value and information in their professional lives.

I am satisfied now as she has accomplished her work with par excellence without losing the essentials of the original content.

My intentions while writing the book was only to record my experiences and memories of the difficult; but it is the rich past of this country's history and its struggle over a period of time which lead us to enjoy the wonderful present of fullness and social satisfaction.

Present is the byproduct of the past; therefore, we cannot neglect to understand the historical knowledge which takes us to succeed in our profession and life.

My book gives an insight into various historical aspects that made Abu Dhabi what it is today. With her keen interest and enthusiasm she made it simpler in its readability, content and orientation for the students.

Well done Melanie, and I wish you and the new lot of its readers to become Richer and Richer in all aspects. All the best.

Mohammed Al Fahim
The Author

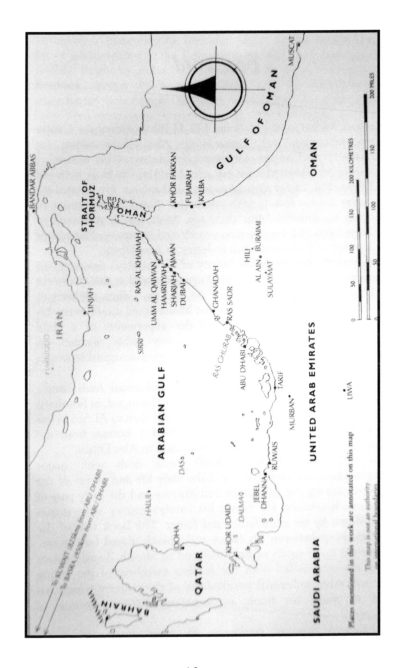

13

Introduction

From Rags to Riches: A Story of Abu Dhabi, Student Edition, is a must read for all young Emiratis. To quote H.H. the late great Sheikh Zayed Bin Sultan Al Nahyan, founder of the modern United Arab Emirates, "A nation without a past is a nation without a present or a future." Thus it is the obligation of every citizen to become knowledgeable about the past so they can know who they are in the present and decide what they want to be in the future. From Rags to Riches tells the story of Abu Dhabi from the pre-oil era until the 1990s through the eyes of local businessman, Mohammad Al Fahim, who grew up in Abu Dhabi and Al Ain in the 1950s and 60s. Mr Al Fahim has documented a very important time period in the history of the UAE through the eyes of his childhood in the Emirate of Abu Dhabi and his knowledge of the people and the region. He writes of the poverty of the one-room school house coupled with the shared sense of community of the people, the harsh trips across the desert by camel caravan from Abu Dhabi to Al Ain paired with the arrival of the first automobiles on desert sands without roads, the novelty and wonder of his first airplane flight from Das Island coupled with the death of his mother in childbirth due to a lack of hospitals and qualified medical staff. Amber Haque, PhD, Associate Professor of Psychology at United Arab Emirates University, writes that, "The young will, of course, model their elders," and calls From Rags to Riches: A Story of Abu Dhabi "an excellent resource on identity and national legacy for the local youth" that should "actually be a part of course curriculum at the undergraduate level for all college students."* This Student Edition has been simplified into graded English for English Language Learners by Dr Patrick Dougherty. Dr Dougherty has been a high school and university educator for more than twenty years in the United States, Japan, Bangladesh, and the United Arab Emirates. He has written two English textbooks, more than twenty monographs and articles, edited three collections of prose and poetry, and is a published short story writer and poet. The simplification of From Rags to Riches, Student Edition was made possible by a grant from the Emirates Foundation (#2009/182).

From the editor, Student Edition

*Haque, A. (2007). Preserving cultural identity in the 21st century: Challenges to the Emirati youth.
Journal of Social Affairs, 24, 13-31.

Chapter 1- **Humble Beginnings**

The Trucial States

The United Arab Emirates (UAE) is made up of seven emirates. They are Abu Dhabi, Dubai, Sharjah, Ras al Khaimah, Umm al Qawain, Fujairah and Ajman. They occupy an area of 77,700 square kilometres. The UAE is bordered by Qatar and Saudi Arabia to the west and south. Oman is to the east. It is separated from Iran by the Arabian Gulf. It had a population of 1,500,000 in the early 1990s. One-third of the population was Emirati. The rest were foreign workers. These were mostly from other Arab countries, Iran, and Asia.

Though small, the UAE is now famous. This is due to its oil. The UAE has played an important part in the energy markets since the 1970s. Before 1971, the situation was different. The UAE did not exist as a country. The area did not have an official name. It was known as the "Pirate Coast." In 1853, the area became known as the "Trucial States."

In the early 1800s the population was 72,000. Ras al Khaimah, Sharjah, Dubai and Abu Dhabi were small villages. Fishermen, pearl divers, and traders lived there. They all depended on the sea for their income. The local food supply was fish, dates, and camel's milk.

The locals traded pearls for imports. Everything, from food to cloth, was imported. They traded with other Gulf neighbors, East Africa and India. Decisions on what to trade and who to trade with were made by the local rulers.

These rulers were called sheikhs.

At the beginning of the 1800s, the Trucial States were composed of three sheikhdoms: Abu Dhabi, Ras al Khaimah, and Sharjah. Abu Dhabi was the largest of the sheikdoms. To the east was Dubai. To the west were Qatar and Saudi Arabia. Finally, to the south was the Sultanate of Oman. Abu Dhabi had three main areas where people lived. They were the island of Abu Dhabi and the oases of Al Ain and Liwa.

The people of Abu Dhabi led very simple lives. There was only a small village where the city of Abu Dhabi is today. Abu Dhabi was home to several Bedouin tribes. Both the Bedouins and the villagers belonged to the Bani Yas tribe. The Bedouins raised animals. The villagers made money from pearl diving. That was the economy before oil.

Pearling - bitter memories

Until the 1950s, the Gulf was one of the most important pearl producing areas in the world. Abu Dhabi had the largest pearling fleet in the region. There were about 400 boats. The next largest fleet was Sharjah's, with 360 boats. Dubai had 335 boats. Pearls were one of the reasons Europeans first came to Abu Dhabi.

The fleets set out in June and did not return until September. The pearl divers were separated from their families for the entire time. Life aboard a pearling boat was not comfortable. The boats were loaded with diving equipment, food supplies, and water. There was no room for the men to sit or sleep. The sun beat down, and the days were long and difficult. The humidity and heat were terrible. Pearl divers dove for up to twelve hours each day. They dove constantly throughout the day. They only stopped to catch their breaths.

A diver's equipment included a bag for oysters, a clip for his nose, and a rope tied around his waist. The rope allowed him to be pulled up after each dive. The dives lasted for two minutes. During that time, a diver could get a dozen oysters. He took them from the sandbank. The sandbank was about twenty meters below. Divers paused for only a minute between each dive. Diving was dangerous. If a diver surfaced too quickly, he could damage his ears or brain. If he was too slow, he might drown. There were also sharks.

Each evening, the oysters were opened and searched for pearls. After this, the men would eat their one meal of the day. Diving was impossible on a full stomach. The men had to wait until evening to eat. Many men lost all their teeth because they did not have enough food. They ate only small rations of dates, rice, and fish. Fresh water was supplied only occasionally. The weather could also be bad. Sometimes the wind blew so hard they were prevented from diving. Sometimes there was no wind. Then the men had to row the heavy boats. It was hard work.

They were only paid when the pearling season was over.

Ten per cent of the money went to the ship owner. Twenty per cent paid for supplies. The remaining seventy per cent was divided. The captain got three shares. The divers and helpers each got one share. The ruler, or sheikh, got one share from each boat in the fleet. Sometimes the divers were paid extra if they found a large pearl, but this rarely happened.

It was a hard life, but the people of Abu Dhabi had little choice. Pearling was their only source of income. It was the only way they could feed their families. Because of this, most people lived simple lives. They had few comforts. They had little hope for the future.

Bare essentials

Most people lived in houses built from the branches of date palm trees. This type of housing was used until the late 1960s. There was no such thing as running water and electricity. People used wood as fuel for their cooking fires. Water came from wells. Wells were often located some distance from the settlement. The water was salty and not clean like today's drinking water. Fresh, clean, water was not available until the 1960s. At that time, the first desalination plant was built. It took the salt out of sea water. This made the water safe to drink.

The women were in charge of the household and the children. Those who were married to fishermen sold the daily catch in the market. The fishermen brought their fish back early in the morning. Their wives took the fish to market to sell or exchange for other things. There were no schools. Children began to work as soon as they were old enough.

Most men had only a simple cloth that they wore around their waists. That was all they wore. They had no shoes or head coverings. Most men wore their hair long to shield against the sun. This changed in the 1960s. The gutra and agal, along with the kandura and the abaya, became common.

Bedouin hospitality - timeless traditions

Caravans travelling in the desert often came upon Bedouin camps. If the travellers were welcomed into the camps, the Bedouin hosts had to protect the caravan. What would happen if the Bedouin offered coffee? The Bedouin would protect the caravan until it was out of sight. Eating a meal? The Bedouin protected them for one day. Staying the night? The Bedouin had to take care of them for three days. Travellers were safe in the desert through this system of hospitality. What did the Bedouin get in exchange? The caravan would purchase supplies from them.

Friendship also played a big role. In those days, the population was so small everyone knew each other. Before you neared a camp, they could tell who you were. If an enemy approached, he would not be allowed in the camp. A traveller would never be offered coffee by the Bedouin until they decided he was welcome.

Traditions such as these were the basis of everyday life less than fifty years ago. People lived by them and sought understanding of the world through them.

Sheikh Zayed bin Khalifa and the British

The Sheikhdom of Abu Dhabi had grown in size and strength in the nineteenth century. It reached a peak under Zayed bin Khalifa, who became leader at the age of twenty. During the first fifteen years of Sheikh Zayed bin Khalifa's fifty-four year rule, he became the most important ruler in the area.

Sheikh Zayed bin Khalifa had plans to unite the area under his own rule. Unfortunately, this never happened. He had many disagreements with the British. They would not let him become the head of the whole area.

Several things led to problems between Sheikh Zayed and the British. First, in 1895, he expressed his intention to build a settlement on the island of Zora for his father-in-law, Sheikh Nasir bin Salmin. The Sheikh of Ajman protested to the British. The British, in turn, pressured Zayed to abandon his plan.

Then, in 1896, Sheikh Zayed bin Khalifa encouraged the French. He established commercial and political relations with them. He offered Abu Dhabi as a port of call for their ships. Two years later, the Sultan of Muscat gave the French a coal depot at Jissah, south of Muscat. The British threatened the Sultan. Unless he stopped working with the

French, his palace would be destroyed. The Sultan agreed. If the British thought a ruler was not going to cooperate, they replaced him with a relative. First in Sharjah, then in Ras al Khaimah, then again in Sharjah, those sheikhs who were critics of the British were removed.

Chapter 2 - Unmet Expectations

Dawn of the twentieth century - troubled waters

At the end of the 1800s, Abu Dhabi was almost the same as it had been a hundred years earlier. Not much progress had been made. In fact, the situation had become worse.

Shipping and trading had been hurt in 1819 when the British destroyed the Qawasim ships. The shipbuilding industry was also destroyed. The people were forced to rely even more on pearl diving.

Abu Dhabi was still a small settlement used mostly to prepare and supply the pearling fleets for the summer. The people of the area were poor. The island village had little to offer. Many people moved to the oases of Al Ain and Liwa. In the oases there were farms and date trees. Even the ruler spent most of his time in Al Ain.

Most of the northern areas were in the same position as Abu Dhabi. Their economies were bad, life was simple, and the outlook for progress and growth was bad. The exception was Dubai, which began to flourish after 1902.

From the 1870s Sunni Arab businessmen and traders living on the Persian coast and nearby islands found it increasingly difficult to live under the control of the Persian government in Tehran. They were seeking better prospects, so they moved to Dubai. Persia's loss was Dubai's gain. These immigrants had strong business relationships with merchants in India.

When they settled in Dubai, they brought with them their knowledge, ambition, and business contacts. In 1902, for the first time, a ship bypassed the Persian coastal city of Linjah. Linjah had been the main trading post for all incoming ships from India. The ship went, instead, to Dubai. In this way, the traders avoided Persian taxes.

The standard of living in Dubai improved. More ships stopped there to unload their goods. Two major factors held Abu Dhabi back during the early years of the twentieth century. The first was the internal power struggle between members of the ruling family. The second was the First World War.

Abu Dhabi had been ruled peacefully for over fifty years by Sheikh Zayed bin Khalifa. When he died in 1909, his son Sheikh Tahnoun took over. Sheikh Tahnoun ruled for only three years before he also died. He was succeeded by his brother, Hamdan bin Zayed, who ruled until 1922. In 1922, Hamad bin Zayed was killed by his brother, Sheikh Sultan. This was after a decade of disagreement. Only five years later, in 1927, Sheikh Sultan was also assassinated by another brother, Saqr. Saqr was killed the following year by another brother's bodyguard. It was a dangerous time to be the sheikh.

This decade-long family conflict was based on greed. It was also encouraged by the British. When a British ship arrived in the Gulf, for example, the ruler would often visit it in a small boat and be seen bringing back a box. Members of his family thought that this box contained money, but it held only papers. The family thought the ruler was keeping money for himself. However, when a safe belonging to one of the dead rulers was opened, it contained only one coin. The British never paid any money to the rulers. Nevertheless, if family members did not trust a ruler, they often turned against him.

The British used tribal and family conflict to their advantage. If a ruler did not support them, they would help to get rid of him. They wanted rulers who would agree with their policies.

The frequent changes in leadership during the first part of the twentieth century left Abu Dhabi floating aimlessly. Abu Dhabi did not become peaceful again until 1928 when Sheikh Shakhbut bin Sultan took over. Because of the constant instability in Abu Dhabi between 1909 and 1928, there was little development. In addition, progress was slowed by the First World War.

During the First World War, there were fewer large ships travelling between Bahrain and Abu Dhabi. This cut off the much needed dates which fed the people in Abu Dhabi. They became even more dependent on what was grown in the oases of Liwa and Al Ain. The demand often exceeded the supply. This resulted in food shortages and hunger. The war also reduced the demand for pearls which affected the Gulf pearl industry. It was a very difficult period for the locals.

The Shakhbut years

There was renewed hope when Sheikh Shakhbut took over in 1928. He was confident that the British would support him. The locals were optimistic, too. They prayed that the sheikh would improve their lives. Sheikh Shakhbut was only twenty-four when he became ruler. People believed his youth and energy would help improve the area. The First World War was over. Peace was established and trade was resuming between the western nations. The pearl industry had recovered a little. At last Abu Dhabi looked forward to a better tomorrow. There was an opinion that the bad days were over. Sadly this was not to be the case.

Sheikh Shakhbut found that the British were not prepared to assist him. Most sheikhs had expected the British to assist them to help their people. They were all disappointed. Shakhbut was no exception. His rule, which ended in 1966, was a difficult one due to a bad economy. The Second World War, threats to the borders, and continuing disputes with the British made economic progress difficult. This was also the time that the pearl industry stopped almost completely.

The end of pearling in the Gulf came in the 1930s. Following the First World War, the Japanese began growing cultivated pearls, which resulted in a huge drop in the price of Gulf pearls. This led to a complete collapse of the pearling industry in the Gulf. Abu Dhabi had to wait twenty years before things changed for the better. Only when oil was found in the region were there new employment opportunities.

The race is on

With the shipping of oil from Bahrain in 1932, interest in the region's oil grew. In 1935, the area leaders signed oil exploration agreements. They received money for these agreements. With the income, Sheikh Shakhbut decided to build Abu Dhabi's first palace. It was a large project that lasted for about four years. The palace project used most of Abu Dhabi's ships to import building materials from across the Gulf. In addition, almost all the men of the area were employed on its construction. This generated income for the locals from 1936 to 1939. However, it was not enough to help people now that the pearl industry was dead.

At the same time, the British oil companies began asking the rulers for agreements giving them exclusive rights to any oil that was found. The Ruler of Dubai signed an agreement in May 1937. The Ruler of Sharjah followed. The rulers of Ras al Khaimah and Kalba agreed in 1938.

Sheikh Shakhbut waited. He wanted better terms and conditions. In the end, however, he too signed an agreement in 1939. He was paid 300,000 rupees for signing the agreement. It was to be followed by additional income later.

Unfortunately, a few months later the Second World War began. The war led to a period of depression in Abu Dhabi. Nothing further was done about developing the oil sector as the British were preoccupied with the war effort. The demand for Gulf pearls was now non-existent and trade was slow. There were even food shortages. As a result, many people left Abu Dhabi to move to other areas of the Gulf.

High hopes

Prospects for the sheikhdom looked much brighter in the 1950s. Oil exploration was growing and more local people were being employed by the oil companies. When oil was discovered at Murban in December 1959, the people of Abu Dhabi were happy. The hard times were over. Or so they thought.

Meanwhile the British pressured Sheikh Shakhbut to give part of his oil money to help the other sheikhdoms. They wanted him to pay for the expenses of other areas since they had less oil. He thought the British should be supporting the other areas with their own money. He saw no reason to help them.

After three decades of conflict with the British, Sheikh Shakhbut had become mistrustful and cautious. Money from the oil agreements had been paid yearly for almost a decade. However, it was not used to improve the area. The sheikh was unwilling to spend any of the money. He was worried he would need it in the future. He also became stubborn with the oil companies. He forced them to advance him money in ever greater amounts. Nevertheless, he finally agreed to spend four per cent of the oil money to help the other areas.

Even while the treasury filled with oil money, Abu Dhabi remained the most primitive of all the sheikhdoms. In 1960, the inhabitants still lived in poverty. Many people went hungry. There were no hospitals to treat the sick. The first regular school had opened only in 1959. Nevertheless, there were signs of improvement. There was an increase in the number of foreigners in Abu Dhabi. New companies set up camps in the desert and on Das Island. They hired locals to work for them. We all knew oil had been discovered. Yet there was no confirmation of the discovery. Privately, Abu Dhabians had many questions. Was the discovery significant? What would it mean for us? How would our lives change? Who would manage the development that would surely be taking place soon? When would we have hospitals and schools? Publicly, however, no one said a word.

Most of the time it seemed foreigners knew more about what was going on in Abu Dhabi than the Abu Dhabians. It was confusing. However, people were so grateful for jobs that no one said anything.

The months went by. There were no changes. No new government institutions were set up. No hospitals or schools were established. Nothing was done to improve the lives of the people. People became somewhat resigned to the fact that we seemed stuck in the nineteenth century. They began to accept the status quo. As a result, when massive change finally did begin some years later, none of the people were ready for it.

Chapter 3 - **Generations in the Gulf**

A short family history

My family has always lived in the Gulf region. My great-grandfather was the head of an Arab village called Harmoud. Harmoud was in the mountains on the southern coast of Iran. The people of the town were active in trading businesses and farming. When my great-grandfather died in the 1880s, his eldest son, my great-uncle, became the ruler of Harmoud.

In the middle of the 1800s, the government of Persia in Tehran began expanding. Its control reached even the village of Harmoud. My family did not like this expansion of authority from Tehran. Like many of the other Arabs who lived on the coast, my family were forced to obey Tehran. They became citizens of Persia.

My grandfather decided to leave Persia. In the mid-1880s, at the age of fifteen, he crossed the Gulf to Dubai. He continued his education in Sharjah. A few years later he got involved in a trading business. Before long, he opened a shop in the souk. His business was a success. Just before 1900, the Dubai souk burned down. All the shops were destroyed.

At the same time, Abu Dhabi and Delma Islands were becoming important centers for the pearl diving industry, so grandfather decided to move to Abu Dhabi. In about 1905, he married a woman from one of the Bani Yas tribes. My grandfather had four sons and three daughters. He was one of a few men who could read and write in Abu Dhabi.

Most of the local men spent the summer months on Delma Island during the pearl season, while the women and younger children lived in Al Ain. Then, during the winter, they would all gather and live together in Abu Dhabi.

My grandfather's business on Delma Island did well through the 1920s. But then, in 1928, a fire spread through the village and destroyed all the shops and houses. The fire was so bad that the town never recovered. It went from a busy trading center to a small fishing village.

Foreign oil companies were becoming interested in looking for oil during this time. Sheikh Shakhbut signed an agreement with the oil companies in 1935. With the money he received from the oil companies, he decided to build Abu Dhabi's first palace.

My father's friendship with Sheikh Zayed bin Sultan began during this time. Sheikh Zayed was travelling between Abu Dhabi and Al Ain and decided to go part of the way by boat. My father and uncles were transporting rock for the palace by boat. Sheikh Zayed travelled with them on their boat. He got to know my father and was impressed with his skills and education.

My father was one of the few people who could read and write at that time. Sheikh Zayed needed someone who had those skills. He asked my father to join him and his family near Al Ain. My father decided to move to Al Ain where he became one of Sheikh Zayed's closest advisors and friends.

Simple lives

In 1946, several years after he went to Al Ain, my father married my mother. My sister was born in 1947, and I arrived the following year.

Life in Abu Dhabi at the time of my birth was the same as it had been in 1800. It was simple. In 1950, the population of Abu Dhabi was about 2,000 people. People did not want to live on Abu Dhabi Island in the summer because of the heat and humidity. Women and children moved either to Al Ain or the Liwa while the men were out pearl diving from May until September.

Until the late 1950s, none of the few people owned a car. Most people continued to rely on camels. During the 1940s and 1950s, and even as late as the 1960s, my family spent the winter months in Abu Dhabi and the summers in Al Ain. We travelled back and forth by camel in the spring and the autumn.

In the autumn of 1947, about a year before my birth, my grandfather, grandmother, and the women of the family joined a caravan headed from Al Ain to Abu Dhabi. A day into the trip, they had camped for the night in an area called Sulaymat, near where the Al Ain airport is located today. Sometime in the evening my grandmother, who was about fifty-five, felt sick. They laid her down on the ground to rest. In a few hours, she was dead. It was a terrible shock to the whole family. My grandmother had been strong and in good health and her death was completely unexpected. As is required in Islam, they buried her there before the end of the next day and continued on toward Abu Dhabi.

Three days later, in a place called Remah near where Al Hasna is now, my grandfather fell sick and he too died suddenly. There were no other men from our family on the trip. The men in the group got together and performed the burial for my grandfather. Of course, it was not uncommon for people to die making trips across the desert. The causes of such deaths were usually sun stroke or travel fatigue. Still, the death of both parents on one trip was a cruel blow to my aunts. They were completely crushed with grief.

Nevertheless, the caravan moved on and arrived in Abu Dhabi three days later with all the women in mourning. My father and uncles were devastated when they heard the sad news. In their sadness, the whole family could do nothing, but accept the deaths of my grandparents as the will of God. They carried on with their lives living simply and humbly like their friends and neighbours.

At that time, the people on Abu Dhabi Island still lived in barasti huts built of date palm fronds. A few wealthier people and the ruling family lived in earth or clay houses. The ruling sheikh stayed in the palace. The houses were close together for warmth during the cooler months. People built away from the sea. We used mats made from palm fronds as flooring in the tents and huts.

We made do with very little, using the same things for different purposes. The palm mats, for example, were used for sitting, sleeping, and keeping the tent warm. We had no more clothes in winter than we had in summer. When it was cold, the whole family slept close together to keep warm at night. In the summer, we slept outside in the open air. Some nights the humidity was so high, I felt as if I were sleeping in a wet blanket.

A daily struggle

During the winter months in Abu Dhabi town, the women took care of the household. They cooked, cleaned, and cared for the children while the men went fishing. The women sold the fish at the market. They bought things for the house and food with the money. The women also got water from the wells twice a day. They carried the water in goatskin bags or clay pots. The wells were about one kilometer from the town.

There was hardly any food. The people ate rice, fish, yogurt, and dates. The rice was imported through Dubai from India. Fish was caught in the Gulf. Yogurt was made from goat's or camel's milk. Dates were grown locally, but some still had to be imported from Bahrain. We did not get enough to eat as the milk supply was low, and we ate few fruits and vegetables.

Clothing was also simple. The men usually had a single kandura, or long dress, which they wore all the time. The children wore next to nothing. The women had one or two kanduras that they had usually made themselves. No one had any shoes, so we all walked barefoot.

Because people were poor, they usually shared everything. They often ate together in the afternoon following prayer. The men and women gathered in separate groups, usually in the shade of the mosque or someone's home, to share their food. Dates, coffee, or whatever they had cooked over the open fire. If they had a visitor, they might borrow food, so they could serve their guest at home.

There were no hospitals or schools in the 1950s except for the religious school run by the local iman, Mullah Darwish. He was an amazing man who was a teacher and poet. He did his best to educate the young and care for the sick because we had no doctor. Abu Dhabi's first hospital did not open until 1967. Because there was no clinic or hospital, many people died, especially women and children. Many women died while giving birth. My own mother died giving birth in 1962 at the age of thirty.

The British never helped us in the areas of education and health care. They never built a school, a medical clinic, or a mosque.

A young life lost

One morning, my younger brother, who was about six years old at the time, was playing outside our house. He found a small box of matches that he began lighting and throwing on the ground. My little sister went over to pick up one of the matches, and her dress caught fire. She was badly burned in minutes. There were no doctors or medicine for treating anything in Muwayje. There were also no hospitals in nearby Al Ain or Buraimi. The nearest medical clinic was in Sharjah. That was at least a two-day journey away.

The whole family was upset. My little sister was in pain, and there was nothing we could do to help her. Sheikh Zayed lent my father his Land Rover and a driver to take us to Sharjah. My father and mother, I, and my other brothers and sisters all got into the Land Rover and headed across the desert to Sharjah. There was no road other than a sandy track, so we got stuck many times along the way. It took us two days to cover the distance. By the time we arrived in Sharjah, my little sister had already died from the burns.

As late as 1957, there was not a single doctor in Abu Dhabi. Most of the rest of the world had easy access to doctors, medicine, and the latest in medical technology to treat the injured and ill. We had nothing. As a result my family lost a beautiful young child. In fact, many people died or suffered needlessly because of the lack of proper medical care. It was only in 1961 that the first clinic was built in Al Ain, and not until 1967 that a hospital was finally established in Abu Dhabi.

Early school days with Mullah Darwish

When we were in Abu Dhabi, both my older sister and I attended the school run by Mullah Darwish bin Karam. The school day started about 6.00 a.m. and lasted until noon with a breakfast break between eight and nine. I remember being so excited about going to school that I would sleep fully dressed, so as not to waste any time getting ready in the morning. As soon as I woke up, I was out of the house and on my way. My sister and I often raced each other to see who would get there first.

Like the houses in Abu Dhabi town the school was built of palm fronds, a round, one-room shelter. It had no equipment, teaching aids, toilets, or water. Each morning we had to refill a big water container inside the school. We refilled the big container by filling small clay pots at the well and carrying them back to the school until we had enough to last us through the morning. Despite the lack of materials, Mullah Darwish did a good job teaching us.

His teaching style was simple. He sat in the middle of the room facing the door while we sat in the sand or on palm mats in a circle around him. Twenty-five or thirty of us, both boys and girls, sat silently reading the Quran. Our entire education consisted of reading the Holy Book. We read it completely, one page at a time. When we felt confident in our ability, Mullah Darwish would listen to us reading. Once he was satisfied, he allowed us to go on to the next page. When he was busy, the mullah told the older boys to listen to the younger ones and help them along.

Some students stayed on the same page for days at a time. Even the best of us took at least a couple of years to go completely through the Quran. I do not recall anyone completing it in a single school year. The school year normally began in October and ended in May.

Every time a student finished reading the Quran, we would all dress up and pass through the town singing. People would give us sweets, or sometimes even some money for the teacher. It was a big day when any of the students finished the Quran and graduated from the school. The only other highlight of the school year was when the rains came in winter.

As soon as the rain began to fall, our concentration was broken. We knew it would soon mean the closing of the school because of flooding. More often than not, within two or three days of the rain having stopped, the shelter would be full of water. This brief holiday was a welcome break from the routine of reading for several hours each morning six days a week.

The mullah was paid for his work based on the number of students he taught. He was supposed to be paid a quarter of a rupee per student per week. However, many of the students could not pay even that small amount. He taught them anyway. He just told them to bring the money when they could. The richer students, however, paid a rupee every two weeks. In addition, when his or her education was completed, each student was supposed to pay two rupees to the mullah. Despite the small payment, many could not pay this small amount either, so they only gave part of it to him.

After completing this part of their education, some students continued with the mullah to learn how to write. We learned how to write by copying. The mullah wrote a sentence at the top of a page, and we copied it over and over. As our skills improved, Mullah Darwish might write a whole composition for copying. Those of us who were able to study were very grateful for the opportunity to do so. Most of our playmates were denied an education. Because their families were so poor, even the children had to work. At the age of twelve the boys started working with their fathers, learning to either fish, farm, or take care of the animals.

Six-room schoolhouse

In 1959, the British government built a small building which they eventually gave to Sheikh Shakhbut to use as a school. By that time, there were about fifty of us, both boys and girls, being taught the Quran by Mullah Darwish.

The new six-room schoolhouse was not much of an improvement over Mullah Darwish's hut. The building had desks, chairs, and chalkboards, but there was no water, toilets, electricity, or books. We had six rooms, but only one teacher. We had to buy our own exercise books and pencils from the souk. It was several years before we got text books and school supplies. At the new school, we were expected to arrive and leave at set times. This was unlike the Quranic School where we came and went as we pleased.

The school year was also longer. We started in September, and went right through until June which meant we suffered the heat and humidity more at the beginning and the end of the school year. In addition, we were punished if we were absent. At the Quranic School, nobody had bothered to take attendance or find out why we were absent. If we told the Mullah we had a stomach ache and had to drink an herbal medicine to clear the system, we could take our leave. In the new school, however, having to take herbal medicine was not an excuse for being absent.

Mullah Darwish retired from teaching when the new school opened. He became general secretary to the ruler and was kept busy writing letters and issuing passports.

Ahmed Al Khatib, a Palestinian who had been living in Jordan, was his replacement. On the first day of school, he lined us all up one behind the other to determine our ages and names, so he could separate us into three groups - one group per classroom. We tried our best to cooperate, but none of us knew our ages and many of us did not know our full names.

We finally ended up being grouped, not by age, but by our ability to read, write, or identify letters. Each group was assigned to one of the three classrooms. The teacher moved between the rooms all day. He would write sentences on the board for us to copy. Those of us who could write would scratch away in our exercise books as long as the teacher was in the room. Then, as soon as he left to attend to another class, we would abandon our work for horseplay.

We did not learn much during our first year there. Year two was no better as we still did not have any text books, and there continued to be a shortage of supplies.

I am quite sure the teacher wondered why they had invited him to teach. Nobody supported him in his efforts. Worse yet, no one even bothered to provide him with a place to live. He had to sleep in one of the empty rooms at the schoolhouse. On top of all that, there wasn't much food. Whichever way he turned, he faced a struggle to live and teach here. Anyone else would have packed up and left.

The lack of facilities, though bad, was understandable given the times and the attitude many local people had toward education. Most were more concerned about surviving than about sending their children to school.

The ruler himself placed little importance on education. When we moved into the new building, he questioned the need for more teachers. He said that the mullah had managed on his own for many years. Why, he asked, was there suddenly a need for more than one teacher? It took a lot of effort to convince him that we needed three separate teachers because we were in three separate classrooms. It was impossible for one person alone to do the job and do it well.

The British did not encourage the education of the local people because it did not further their own interests. It was not until later, when British companies found they needed locally trained workers, that the oil companies

41

opened the Abu Dhabi Marine Areas (ADMA) industrial training school. It was set up in 1960 to teach students the job-related skills needed to work in the oil fields. The new training school got a lot of boys from the regular school and taught them the basics of oil field work for a few months. Then, the boys were sent to work on Das Island or inland on the oil rigs. In either case, they were poorly paid.

Later, the government took over the schools. Most were closed down because they had opened only to meet the labor needs of the oil companies rather than to meet the educational needs of the local people. It would be many years before the young people of Abu Dhabi could get a decent education.

Good intentions

In 1959, there was a terrible flood in Abu Dhabi. It was not protected by the Corniche as it is today. There was nothing to keep the sea from flooding the town. A storm blew in during the night catching everyone as they slept.

We tried to save what we could. However, it happened so fast that not much could be saved. In no time the water level in the souk was more than a meter high. Every single household on the island was damaged. The only buildings which were saved were the palace and a few houses which stood on high ground. The waters did not go back down for two days. About a week after the flood, a large British ship unloaded some dry blankets and canned food which were given to the local people. It was a very kind and much appreciated gesture.

*Above: Leaving for the UK. Well wishers on the air strip 1964.
I am 4th from the left.*

*Below: The first Abu Dhabian students sent to study in England
– Mohammed Al Duhaim; Mohammed Sultan Al Yousif; Harib
B. Bendoug; Saeed Omran; Yousef Ameri; Mohammed Darwish
Karam; the Author; Hamsa Ameri; Abdullah Al-Fahim; Jumaa
Muhairi.*

Above: The banquet that never was. Waiting, (I am third from right), with my father, for the pig to appear.

Right: My brother and I about to take the train to Weston Super Mare, 1964.

Above: With my British guardian Mr. Brian Jackson.

Right:
Abu Dhabi
girl collecting
drinking
water. 1963.

Below: General view of Abu Dhabi from ADMA offices, 1962.

Above: Travelling on camel back was the only form of transport before 1960.

Below: The souk - Abu Dhabi town, 1962.

Above: With the introduction of cars in 1961, petrol was brought to Abu Dhabi in steel drums.

Below: Abu Dhabi's first airport, 1961.

Above: A Gulf Aviation (DC3) on Abu Dhabi's air strip, 1961.

Below: Bedouin encampment in the desert.

Above: National Day celebration at Al Ahli Sport club, 1968.

Below: The author speaking to Special Care Centre, 2002.

Above: The Eid prayer after Ramadan, 1962.

Below: At an official gathering, from left: Col. J. E. H. Boustead, political agent; Saleem Ali Moosa, Agency Interpreter; Sheikh Shakhbut Bin Sultan, Ruler; Mohammed B. Khalifa Al Nahyan; Sheikh Zayed Al Nahyan, Ruler of Eastern Province.

Above: The women of Abu Dhabi selling fish and produce in the souk, 1961.

Left: The Ruler's Palace – The Old Fort, dominates the Abu Dhabi skyline, 1961.

Above: As children we wanted to be like Sheikh Zayed.

Above: Tracks in the sand approaching Abu Dhabi town, 1954.

Above: Desalinated water still had to be poured into cans and loaded on to donkeys for the journey home, 1963.

Below: Fishermen mending their nets.

Above: Abu Dhabi seashore and main centre of activity, 1960.

Below: The seashore, now the corniche of today.

Above: My father (centre) with his next door neighbour Sheikh Tahnoon (left) and Sheikh Mubarak (right), 1994.

Below: From left my father, my uncles Ahmed and Abdul Rahim, my brother Abdullah with me, 1993.

Above: First school students in Abu Dhabi, 1960.

Below: First school in Abu Dhabi (shoeless students), 1961.

Above: Our dream project " The Holiday Centre" complex.

Above: A friendship that spanned more than fifty years.
My late father (left) with the late Sheikh Zayed.

Above: A word of wisdom from Sheikh Zayed to the author.

Above: The town of Abu Dhabi with its barasti houses and first main road, 1961.

Below: Abu Dhabi children, 1958.

Chapter 4 - **Mixed Blessings**

Oil

Without the development of the oil industry, Abu Dhabi would not look any different from one hundred years ago. Oil, or "black gold," as it is often called, has been important in the Gulf region for a long time.

The British cleverly re-confirmed the agreements they had signed with the sheikhs in 1892. The sheikhs agreed not to give oil contracts to any foreigner without the permission of the British. In 1935, Petroleum Concessions Ltd (PCL) established an office in Bahrain to handle oil contracts in the region. In 1936, PCL created Petroleum Development (Trucial Coast) - PD (TC). Later, it asked the sheikhs for agreements giving the company the right to explore for oil in their lands.

The Ruler of Dubai was the first to agree in May 1937. He was followed by the Ruler of Sharjah. He signed an agreement in September of the same year. In December of the following year, PD (TC), later to become the Abu Dhabi Company for Onshore Oil Operations (ADCO), signed agreements with the Rulers of Ras al Khaimah and Kalba. The Ruler of Abu Dhabi held out a little longer. He signed an agreement in January 1939. He got 300,000 Indian rupees for signing, 100,000 rupees yearly when they were exploring for oil, and then 200,000 rupees every year once oil was found. He would receive an additional three rupees for every ton of oil that was exported. The agreement was for seventy-five years.

When the Second World War started in 1939, oil exploration stopped until 1946. Three years later, the first oil well was drilled at Ras Sadr, about fifty kilometers from Abu Dhabi Island. After more than a year of drilling, the well was found to be dry. The second well was drilled at Murban, about 100 kilometers southwest of Abu Dhabi Island. It and several others were found to be dry. Drillers returned to Murban in 1958 where they finally struck oil in 1959.

In the meantime, another concession in Abu Dhabi's waters was awarded in 1953. Abu Dhabi Marine Areas (ADMA) was formed to look for oil offshore in the seabed. The headquarters of ADMA was located at Das Island, a small island about sixty kilometers from Abu Dhabi.

Oil was found in the seabed in 1958. The first shipment of oil left Das Island four years later in July 1962. Eighteen months later, in December 1963, the first shipment from the onshore field at Bab was exported from Jebel Dhanna. Although the early years of the oil industry were very successful, they were not without difficulties for the people of Abu Dhabi.

Empty promises

With the decline of the pearl industry from the early 1930s, life in Abu Dhabi had grown increasingly hard. When oil exploration, then drilling, began in the late 1930s, things finally started looking up. With the discovery of oil ten years later, there seemed to be a light at the end of the tunnel. However, the early days of the oil industry were only a little better than the years before. Local people working for the oil companies hardly earned any money. None got rich.

As the oil business picked up again after the war, more local people found jobs with the oil companies. Thankful for the opportunity to work, they took any job they could get. Most were cleaners, watchmen, drivers, and cooks. The better jobs went to Indians or Arabs from Lebanon, Syria, and Palestine. While foreigners were the supervisors, the local people performed the hard work. They were often paid less than three rupees per day. The local people had bad housing as well as poor food and bad working conditions. Life in the camps was better for the foreigners. They lived comfortably in good housing and ate good food. The local workers, on the other hand, slept in tents, or under the stars and were fed little more than rice and lentils.

Because of the poor conditions, there was always trouble between the local workers and the company supervisors. The ill feelings sometimes even affected the Bedouin people who lived near the company camps. One story is told of some bedu who went to one of the camps to ask for some food. The company supervisors refused. They chased the bedu away telling them never to return. That night the bedu crept silently back to the camp. The next morning the supervisors woke to find themselves without a tent! The bedu were so quick and quiet in taking the tent that the supervisors slept straight through.

In 1966, when Sheikh Zayed became the Ruler of Abu Dhabi, one of his first acts was to meet with the oil companies and make new agreements. He wanted to improve conditions for his people. From then on, things began to turn around. The relationship between the foreign oil companies and the local people improved.

The future looks brighter

As the oil industry began to expand in the late 1950s, so did the importance of Abu Dhabi town as a trading and commercial center.

While the local population was increasing slowly, the number of foreigners was increasing rapidly. Abu Dhabi needed to develop much faster than it was. Almost daily, the oil companies brought in more people. There were no restaurants, nor was there any housing. We did not even have a hotel in Abu Dhabi at the time. The first hotel opened in 1962.

For the most part, the local people welcomed the arrival of foreigners. The local people took advantage of the situation. Some people rented parts of their homes. Others managed to buy a car or pickup and rent them to the foreign companies.

Daring desert driving

Motorized vehicles - mostly ex-army trucks and four-wheel drives - had begun to appear in Abu Dhabi in the late

1950s. They were very popular, especially with members of the ruling family who were more able to afford to buy them at the time.

Over time, transportation by camel, horse, and donkey became less common. Those who owned cars drove them wherever they could. As they drove, they turned and swerved to avoid getting stuck in the sand. These early driving habits can be seen in old photographs where tire tracks crisscross in a million different directions.

It was easier to drive in the desert. The ground was harder there than on the island of Abu Dhabi where the sand was soft and deep. All cars had special balloon sand tires, so they could move at all. Once a vehicle got stuck, it was tough to get it out. Most drivers carried metal sheets and steel plates as well as shovels. They used these under the tires if the car got stuck.

Although there was no road from the town to the edge of the island until 1961, there was a small bridge at Maqta from 1952 onwards. It was made of stone and mud and stood about two feet above the water level, so both cars and camels could easily cross the channel.

Though still very young, I was interested in the motorized vehicles and was eager to learn how to drive. A twenty-three year old cousin in Al Ain owned a vehicle. He had purchased a Land Rover for his own use. Because he was the only one in the family with transportation, he was expected to rise early in the morning, go to the date palm grove, gather the dates required for the day, and bring them back to the village before seven o'clock in the morning. My cousin, who preferred his sleep to this pre-dawn trip, was quite happy to allow me to perform this early morning chore for him. Unfortunately, he refused to let me drive after sunrise. While he slept, I was free to take the Land Rover. However, as soon as he awoke, I had to give him back the Land Rover until the next morning. Nevertheless, I have him to thank for allowing me to learn how to drive at the age of thirteen!

Heaven on earth

In the early 1960s, airline routes were established between Abu Dhabi and Sharjah and Abu Dhabi and Bahrain by Gulf Aviation, which later became Gulf Air. Old Second World War planes, carrying eight to twelve passengers, were used on the first regularly scheduled flights in and out of Abu Dhabi. The flights were always full. It was a struggle to make a reservation, let alone get on the planes that took off and landed from a stretch of sabkha, or salt flat, which was the airport. I experienced the airport when I took my first trip off the shores of the Abu Dhabi mainland in 1961.

Two of my uncles lived and worked on Das Island. My first adventure away from home was a visit to the two of them. I left Abu Dhabi by boat one afternoon, travelled through the night, and arrived early the next morning as the sun came up. Das Island was farther ahead in modern facilities than Abu Dhabi. I stayed with my uncle in a room which had an electric lamp and a fan. There was an open-air cinema where the audience watched recent English films sitting in chairs instead of in the sand. The whole place was amazing to me. Everything was new and seemed so advanced. They had piped water, showers, and towels. I had never owned a towel. Here there were towels for everyone. All of these things were unheard of in Abu Dhabi. I was impressed by the modern way of life enjoyed on Das Island.

I decided then and there that this was the place for me. It was like heaven on earth, so far beyond the reality of my daily life that I could hardly believe that it was not a dream. I asked my uncle if I could stay there with him and work in the restaurant. I was ready to work as a tea boy or a shop helper if it meant that I could continue living on the island. But, I was only thirteen at the time, so my uncle turned me down.

If the visit to Das Island was like a dream come true, the trip home was one of the highlights of my youth. I flew high above the waters and islands of the Gulf in one of the Gulf Aviation airplanes, amazed by the cream-colored shores and turquoise water below. The return trip took only a fraction of the time it had taken to get there of course.

Two steps forward, one step back

The events of 1961 were driven by the discovery of significant oil deposits the previous year on Das Island. While the British were well informed about the developments of the oil industry, the local people were kept in the dark. There may not have been much official news, but we could see that some things were beginning to change.

In February 1961, Abu Dhabi's first desalination plant began producing drinkable water. It was a great leap forward for the community. We expected to have all the fresh water we could use. Unfortunately, the water produced was bad. The plant did not have the chemicals to clean the water. But, it was the only sweet water we had, so we drank it anyway.

During the several months it took to get the first plant up and running, the Ruler ordered a second desalination plant which arrived in August. Unfortunately, the suppliers failed to provide enough pipes to reach the sea, so the plant was useless for a long time. In fact, I do not recall it ever producing any fresh water at all.

These two plants, one without the proper chemicals and the other without enough pipelines to reach the sea, were examples of projects gone wrong. In addition to the problems with the plants themselves, two other factors dampened our excitement over the new water supply. First, we had to pay for whatever we used.Secondly, we still faced the task of hauling the water either by ourselves or with the help of a donkey, as few local people had motorised vehicles at the time. Even those who had cars had difficulty getting to the desalination plant that worked without getting stuck, as it was surrounded by deep soft sand. There was no road or even a hard-packed track approaching the plant.

During the spring and summer of 1961, the Ruler took a long trip overseas. While he was away, Sheikh Zayed built Abu Dhabi's first road. It stretched from the palace to where the Maqta Bridge now stands on the way out of town.

On the educational front, the Ruler asked my father and Khalifa bin Yousef, another businessman from Abu Dhabi, to go to Jordan in search of school teachers to staff the two-year-old school which had been managed until then by a single teacher. My father and Khalifa bin Yousef flew to Jordan in the autumn where they met with King Hussein. He was kind enough to instruct his Minister of Education to help them find teachers. In spite of the low salary, they managed to hire about ten teachers.

Bahraini visitors

The Kanoos were interested in establishing an Abu Dhabi office to represent the shipping side of their business. Once here, they found that in order to begin, they first had to get permission from the Ruler. Given the Ruler's dislike of signing almost anything, they had a difficult time of it. Sheikh Shakhbut finally signed an agreement with the Kanoos with the help of my father.

Several members of the Kanoo family stayed at our home. We had no electricity, running water, or toilets. They slept inside on the floor in the afternoons and outdoors on the roof of my cousin's clay shelter at night. As they had been educated in England, they were used to far more comforts.

Living our simple existence must have been difficult for them, but the Kanoos accepted our hospitality.

Paradise Found

If I had been impressed with Das Island, I was completely overwhelmed by Bahrain. The whole atmosphere was futuristic compared to Abu Dhabi. Bahrain's development had progressed much faster than ours. While we had established our first and only non-religious school in 1959, their first school had opened nearly forty years earlier in 1921. They had hospitals in the 1920s and roads and traffic police as far back as 1930. When we visited in 1961, Bahrain had running water and electricity. We lived in the eighteenth century while the rest of the world, even our neighbors, lived in the twentieth century. We had nothing to offer visitors and nothing to export. We had no importance to the outside world whatsoever.

My father decided to start importing and selling spare parts for automobiles. He travelled to Bahrain where he planned to buy automotive parts which he felt would sell in Abu Dhabi. My brother and I were lucky enough to go with him on this buying trip. It was my second experience on a Gulf Aviation plane, and I was just as thrilled the second time around as I had been the first.

Visiting Bahrain was like taking a trip to another planet. Everything was modern. They even had hotels, one of which we stayed in, with air-conditioned rooms and comfortable dining areas. The souk was vast and busy, with all kinds of items which we had never seen in the Abu Dhabi market. Everything we saw in Bahrain was new and exciting.

During the short time we were in Bahrain, my father bought everything he needed to open the automotive shop. After the trip, it was difficult for my brother and me to accept the simple lifestyle we had at home. We could no longer sleep on the floor without thinking of the room we had in Bahrain. We could no longer bathe without thinking how pleasant it was to shower in the clear water of Bahrain. Everything we did we compared with how much better it was in Bahrain.

Chapter 5 - **The Threshold of Development**

Castles in the sand

In 1962, there was slow, but steady progress in Abu Dhabi. The first oil shipment was exported during the summer. Despite this achievement, Abu Dhabi continued to take only small steps toward development.

Throughout 1962, and over the next few years, the British continued trying to get Sheikh Shakhbut to start the improvements that would allow Abu Dhabi to grow. The British Political Agency put together a development plan for the town. Engineers and consultants arrived full of ideas and plans. Everything was in place. Naturally, the British stood to gain greatly from the development of Abu Dhabi. British companies would do the work. Abu Dhabi stood to gain a great deal as well.

Sheikh Shakhbut, however, remained on bad terms with the British. He did not like anything they suggested. This was frustrating for the British authorities, but the people of Abu Dhabi suffered, too. The need for housing, supplies, and services continued to increase. Since the oil companies' needs could not be met in the local market, they were forced to turn to Bahrain, Qatar, and the United Kingdom for goods and services. There was no benefit to the local economy.

As a result, Abu Dhabi was left far behind in development. Many of the oil field suppliers were located in Dubai. It grew more important as a commercial center and benefited significantly from the oil-related activity in Abu Dhabi.

Unfortunately, Abu Dhabi's growth was affected by the poor relationship between the Ruler and the British.

Worsening relations

As time went on the relationship between Sheikh Shakhbut and the British became worse. Shortly after the first export of 33,000 tons of oil from Das Island in July 1962, the Ruler and Abu Dhabi Marine Areas (ADMA) began arguing over how, and how much, they would pay him. ADMA had a signed agreement stating that he should receive twenty per cent of the sale at the market price. The Ruler, however, felt he should be able to take possession of twenty per cent of the oil shipment, and then sell it at his price. ADMA explained to him the impossibility of his plan. He was furious and blamed the British for his bad relationship with the oil companies.

Meanwhile, the people of Abu Dhabi continued to live simple lives. In the meantime, construction of the town's first real hotel was finished toward the end of the summer. It was called the Abu Dhabi Beach Hotel. The twenty-five room hotel, located near where the Sheraton Hotel stands now, was considered a significant achievement of which Abu Dhabians were very proud. It even had electricity provided by a generator. We sometimes drove there with our father, but their prices were way beyond our means. A soft drink at the hotel cost three rupees - four times the price we paid for a drink at the souk. So the hotel was mostly used by oil companies and other visitors.

Needless loss

While they were important to all Abu Dhabians, the milestones of 1962 were insignificant for my family when compared with the tragic death of my mother in the spring of that year. She was seven months pregnant when she went into labor. There were still no doctors, nurses, clinics, or hospitals in Abu Dhabi. Both my mother and her baby died during the early delivery. She was only thirty. Whenever I remember her death, I am still angered by the fact that we had no proper medical facilities in Abu Dhabi at the time.

Most people around the world, even in the Gulf, had the best in medical services, yet we did not have a nurse, let alone a doctor, in Abu Dhabi. Either our government or the British could have built a hospital. Instead of benefiting from proper health care, our lives were made more difficult. People died from treatable diseases and fever because those who had the power to change things were either unwilling or too mean to do so.

The Arab voice

In the following year, 1963, we again took a few more small steps forward in the slow march of progress. There were three major developments in the area of communications. The first post office opened, the number of battery-operated radios increased, and a telephone system was installed.

The town's first post office opened in March thus speeding up the mail service between Abu Dhabi and the rest of the world. The second, and perhaps the most important in terms of the well-being of the people, was the increase in the number of radios in Abu Dhabi. Most of them were "battery-operated" because we still had no electricity at the time. People began to listen to Radio Cairo, the voice of the Arab world. As they listened, they started to realize there was a world beyond the shores of Abu Dhabi, a world full of countries more advanced than ours.

Partly as a result of the radio coverage, as well as other events which were taking place in the rest of the Arab world, some of the local oil workers in Abu Dhabi went on strike in 1963. In comparing their pay with that of workers elsewhere, Abu Dhabians employed with the oil companies found their salaries to be low. There were work stoppages in Jebel Dhanna, Tarif, and Das Island as local workers demanded better pay and working conditions. Living conditions for all workers were improved.

Few amusements

Youngsters growing up in Abu Dhabi had to be very imaginative in finding things to pass the time. We did not play any sports to speak of. We had no facilities and no one to teach us how to play games such as football. Our first school sports day consisted of contests requiring little equipment. The event was held next to the grand mosque on flat ground. We competed in running, jumping, and tug-of-war. On Fridays and holidays, we spent most of the day either swimming or playing on the beach. In the late afternoon, we would play hide-and-seek until dusk turned into the night and we could no longer see where to run or hide. Aside from school, the sea, and our simple games, there were few other amusements

I was lucky. I had been given a bicycle by my uncle when I was about fourteen. Three or four of my friends had managed to get bikes, too. We rode our bikes together in the souk. It was the only place with a surface hard enough for cycling. The shopkeepers sprayed water on the sand pathway, so people could walk in between the shops more easily. This also made the pathways perfect for bike riding. My last childhood memories of the early 1960s are of the simple lives we lived.

We worked very hard to get a coin or two from our relatives. I remember asking my father for some money one day as he left for Al Ain on one of his many trips. He reached in his pocket to draw out a single rupee, telling me it was the last one he had. But he gave it to me all the same. When I remember my father giving me that coin, I think of the vast differences between our lives then and now.

Despite the huge changes, some of the traditions of my childhood live on. Youngsters today are still given gifts at Eid just as we were then at the end of Ramadan or during the Haj period. We went from house to house to gather either sweets and chocolates, or coins. Sometimes we were given canned milk, brought over from Das Island. Apart from that, we had few treats. Because sweets were relatively scarce, people often gave us money at the Eid when they could spare it. If we were lucky, they would give us a fraction of a rupee. After three days of visiting the neighbors' houses, we might end up with five rupees in our pocket. This was a fortune to us. However, we would quickly spend it by buying whatever candies and things we found at the souk. We often spent all our money in less than a day.

A dream comes true

By 1964 there was a lot of hope. The first oil income payments had actually been paid and amounted to over four million pounds. It was only natural that some of this income should find its way to the people. People remained hopeful that great change was just around the corner. However, they were poorly equipped to deal with what was to come. Only a few people could read or write. They looked to their children to carry them into the future. They began to understand the importance of education.

My father and my family were more fortunate than most. At the beginning of the year, the British Political Agent in Abu Dhabi was interested in sending some of the younger boys to the UK to study English over the summer. The person he contacted, a Mr Brian Jackson from Maidenhead in England, was so interested when he heard about the project that he decided to come to Abu Dhabi and see the place for himself. He arrived sometime in February or March. During his visit, he interviewed possible students. My name, as well as my brother Abdullah's, had been given to him. When he came to Abu Dhabi, he stopped by my father's shop to meet us. My father was willing to send both of us, but he could not afford all the expenses which included return flights, school fees, and pocket money. As it happened, Sheikh Zayed was in Abu Dhabi at the time, and my father told him about his problem. Sheikh Zayed immediately offered to pay for the airline tickets if my father paid for the school fees.

That is how my brother and I came to set off for England in the spring of 1964. We left Abu Dhabi from the salt flat area that still served as the town's airport, on one of the weekly Gulf Aviation flights to Bahrain, and then we travelled on to England.

Mr Jackson met us at Heathrow airport, and then put us on a train to Weston-super-Mare where we stayed with a lovely family who had children our age. Everything was new to us. I had had very little contact with foreign families and the British way of life. We had to learn almost everything. First, how to eat with a knife and fork, and then how to appreciate the different types of food we were offered. The family we stayed with was kind and understanding and took very good care of us. Despite their kindness and best efforts, however, both my brother and I were terribly homesick. We missed our father, our brothers and sisters, our cousins, and our aunts and uncles. We wanted to go back to Abu Dhabi.

But my father insisted in his letters that we should stay and start school in September. He advised Mr Jackson who then made arrangements for me to go to a school in Lincolnshire while my brother was sent to Westgate-on-Sea in Kent. It was a new experience for both of us. We learned how to behave like our fellow students. As it turned out, it was a great experience, and we had a lot of fun.

Dust in the wind

In our dreams, we hoped to find Abu Dhabi reborn like a butterfly, a beautiful shining city freed from its dusty desert cocoon. But our own expectations were way out of line with the reality of what had happened, or rather, with what had not happened during our absence.

I was travelling alone as my brother Abdullah had left England before me. I made what I thought would be my last transit stop in Bahrain, only to discover there was no onward flight to Abu Dhabi because the runway was flooded with rainwater. No landings were possible until the strip was either pumped dry or dried on its own. I waited a week in Bahrain during which I was in constant contact with Gulf Aviation. They finally suggested that I take an oil company plane to Tarif where I could be picked up and driven to Abu Dhabi. The oil company kindly agreed to let me have a seat on their plane. I was met in Tarif by a friend, Sulaiman Khansaheb, whose father was responsible for building the first bridge between Abu Dhabi Island and the mainland in 1952. He drove me to the bridge at Maqta in his Land Rover where I was greeted by my father and my brother. They had brought me a wonderful gift, my first car. It was a used 1964 sky-blue Chevrolet saloon car with the balloon tires necessary for driving in Abu Dhabi. I was thrilled with the gift which I drove proudly into town on the mud road built by order of Sheikh Zayed in 1961.

However, my delight with the car soon turned to disappointment when I found that nothing at all had changed at home. Everything was exactly as I had left it. There was still no electricity, and people continued to live in huts made out of palm fronds.

Once back in Abu Dhabi, I was a little like a fish out of water. Returning to the local school was out of the question. I had already learned more during my six months in England than my classmates would learn in the next two years. Instead of going back to school, I began helping my father in his spare parts shop. But, after a few months, my father told me that it would better for me to go back to England to further my education.

I returned to Lincolnshire for the spring term in 1965 to continue school. After graduating in 1966, I worked at the Ottoman Bank in London for nine months. During that time, I was given the responsibility, with Mr Jackson, of looking after several other young Abu Dhabi boys who had come to England to study. By the time I left England, the following year, an office in London took over the supervision of the students. I flew back to Abu Dhabi in 1967. This time when I landed, the transformation the local people and I had dreamed of for so many years was finally beginning to occur.

Chapter 6 - **Leaps and Bounds**

An important leader

While I was in England, Sheikh Zayed became the leader of Abu Dhabi on 6 August 1966. We were happy about this. We felt he was the right man for the job. I had known him since I was a young boy.

He was a very brave and strong man. He worked hard at keeping contact with the people of the area around Al Ain and the rest of Abu Dhabi. He helped them with their problems whenever he could.

Sheikh Zayed liked to meet the families of those around him. He always put himself in the shoes of those he met, particularly if they were in need. Then he went out of his way to help them if he could. His strength and courage were always matched by his kindness, particularly with children. He made them feel comfortable by asking their names and speaking with them. As I grew older, I would go to visit him in the palace in Abu Dhabi. I loved to listen to him talk. He was skilled at giving advice. He would speak to everyone, so they could all hear and take advantage of his advice.

Fierce patriotism

Sheikh Zayed believed that oil money should be used to develop Abu Dhabi. Unfortunately his older brother, Sheikh Shakhbut, felt the money should be saved for emergencies. Sheikh Zayed believed that developing the country and educating the local people were more important. As governor of the Al Ain area, he had worked hard to develop the area as much as he could.

Over the next eighteen months, he talked to the ruling family, including his brothers and cousins. They all agreed that the situation could not continue as it was. With the help of the British, a change was finally brought about on 6 August 1966. On that day Sheikh Zayed became the Ruler of Abu Dhabi. The former Ruler, Sheikh Shakhbut went to Bahrain, then to Iran, and finally to Lebanon where he lived for many years.

Starting from scratch

Because his efforts had been frustrated for so long, Sheikh Zayed began his rule with an act of generosity. He opened the palace and gave away all the money that had been saved by the old leader. He announced that anyone in need could come to Abu Dhabi from anywhere in the area to receive money. Although I was not here at the time, I heard stories of long lines in front of the palace as people waited to get a share of the money. Everyone was thankful. With that first act of kindness, the changes began.

When I got back from England a little over a year later, the city was a completely different place from the one I had left. As soon as he was in control, Sheikh Zayed began taking steps that would bring Abu Dhabi into the modern world. The task was difficult. First, he needed to put together an entire government because nothing existed at the time. He was a man who had never been to school, a man who had lived a bedouin life since his youth. Yet, he created the modern day Abu Dhabi.

Record-breaking growth

Now that Sheikh Zayed was in charge, my father's role as his advisor took on even more importance. While he helped Sheikh Zayed realize his plans for Abu Dhabi, my father needed someone to take care of the family business. So he asked me to come back from England. I was looking forward to going on to university, but my father insisted that I return home. I arrived in September in 1967. I was nineteen at the time. When I arrived, a little over a year after Sheikh Zayed had become ruler, the town was rapidly changing. As we drove into Abu Dhabi town from the airport, I was amazed at the transformation. The sleepy fishing village I had left was now a busy construction site.

There were trucks, bulldozers, cars, and people everywhere. They were doing everything from building roads to laying cables. Abu Dhabi was a beehive of activity. There were labor camps everywhere for the workers to live. Commercial buildings, government buildings, housing, warehouses, and shops were all going up at the same time. A whole city was being built from nothing. I was happy. It was an exciting time. We jumped forward two hundred years. We went from "no tech" to "high tech" in a matter of a few years.

Thankfully, many Abu Dhabians who had left in the previous thirty years began to come back after 1966. They brought with them skills and work experience. They became part of the building of a modern community.

No room at the inn

The Beach Hotel which had been opened in 1964 had never been full until 1966. Suddenly it was always fully booked. There was no other place for visitors to stay. The hotel staff was flooded with requests for rooms. They added extra beds in all the rooms. Then they put more in the hallways. They even used part of the dining room for sleeping.

While there was a shortage of rooms for visitors and workers during the late 1960s and early 1970s, the local people were moving from their traditional housing to new homes. The old town, made of palm-frond huts, was being torn down for the modern city. As the huts were torn down to make way for new housing, the local people were given large amounts of money by the government. The money was enough to build a new house and start a small business.

In addition, Sheikh Zayed also gave each local three pieces of land. The first was for a home, the second was to build a commercial building, and the third was for an industrial site to make a factory. In addition to these three plots, the people of Liwa and outlying villages also received a gift of farmland. They were also given the necessary equipment to farm the land including machinery, pumps, and irrigation systems. Even engineers and consultants from the department of agriculture were provided free of charge.

These land grants were important in teaching many locals how to become landowners and landlords. They generated a fixed income for themselves and their families by building commercial space at the downtown sites. Then they rented them, or the industrial sites which were rarely used by local businessmen at the time. The policy of giving each Abu Dhabian property on the island of Abu Dhabi continued until the 1980s when the land eventually ran out.

Supportive strategies

Supporting the local people like this was typical of the way in which Sheikh Zayed approached the development of Abu Dhabi. The local people needed his help. They had lived in palm-frond huts for hundreds of years, barely surviving from one year to the next. They had none of the necessary skills to live in a modern society. Sheikh Zayed's foresight was crucial in helping the people move from the past to the present. At the time, many local men were leaving their traditional lifestyles as fishermen, shop keepers, or animal traders. They could see that progress offered opportunities in trading, importing, and exporting. Unfortunately, almost none of them had the education or the experience to get them started.

The government declared that all foreign companies had to be in partnership with a local businessman. This made sure that a certain percentage of the profits went back into the local economy through the local businessmen. The government also declared that no contract would be awarded to any company which was not sponsored by an Abu Dhabian. They also gave preference to those which were majority owned by local businessmen. Additionally, the government made it a policy to order all of its supplies locally. Since the local businessmen were so strongly supported by the government, the banks were quick to offer them credit to help them get established. These strategies went a long way toward building a foundation for an economy which now includes many locally-owned companies.

As might be expected, however, there were problems along the way. The locals were simply not used to having large amounts of money. Some spent their money wisely building new homes and getting involved in business. Others, however, went directly to a car showroom. They used their money to pay cash for new cars. It took time for the locals to understand the value of money. Yet, Sheikh Zayed's efforts paid off. Abu Dhabi's oil wealth has been shared amongst the many rather than just the few.

In the driver's seat

While all of this was going on around me, I was busy learning the family business. In the beginning, my father gave me responsibility for the automotive parts shop. He had also opened a small travel agency. In addition, he had built six small shops for businesses on Sheikh Hamdan Street. At that time, Sheikh Hamdan Street was a small part of the first road that Sheikh Zayed had built.

Most goods from Europe took about three months to get to Abu Dhabi. The city was not a regular stop as there was no port at the time. Once they got here, the goods, including vehicles, were off-loaded from the ships onto flat boats about three or four kilometers from shore. Then they were pulled to the beach.

Cars were driven off the boats onto the beach by driving on pieces of wood. The cars often got stuck in the soft sand and had to be pushed out. As I stood on the beach supervising, customers would come over and ask me the price of the cars. If they found the price acceptable, they would fill my hands with cash and drive away in their new car. There was no paperwork. People just handed me the money, took the keys, and drove off.

Chapter 7 - **Birth of a Nation**

Born of necessity

In January 1968, the British said they were leaving all territories east of the Suez in Egypt. This included Abu Dhabi and the surrounding sheikhdoms. Their decision had effects on the development of the area. It also had a negative impact on the British trade here.

When the British decided to leave, they ended their control of the local market. Soon companies from Japan, France, Germany, Italy, and the United States came to the area. Customers began moving away from British goods as better products came on the market.

British withdrawal from the area also ended the British military protection that had guarded the coastal area since 1892. That opened the door for one of our bigger neighbors, such as Iran or Saudi Arabia, to claim land that was ours. Sheikh Zayed recognized the danger. He proposed to the rulers of the other sheikhdoms that they form a union.

The job of showing the benefits of federation fell to Sheikh Zayed. While he was convinced of the advantages of such a union, the other rulers were less enthusiastic. The men Sheikh Zayed had to convince were the same ones the Abu Dhabi ruling family had been in conflict with for years. Sheikh Zayed had a challenging task ahead of him if he was to get them to accept his proposal. By compromising on the frontier issue between Abu Dhabi and Dubai, Sheikh Zayed managed to convince the ruler of Dubai to join.

Within the following two weeks, the five other rulers of the emirates which now comprise the UAE, as well as the rulers of Qatar and Bahrain, had met and agreed to form a country. The details of the structure of the federation still had to be agreed on, however. Building a proposal to which all the rulers could agree was challenging.

Federation proves challenging

Sheikh Zayed was tireless. He travelled across the region and flew to Bahrain. He invited the ruling sheikhs to meet. He pushed them to forget the past and encouraged them to think ahead. The British were leaving, that was clear. Without their protection, the area was at risk.

Sheikh Zayed never gave up. He even offered the British money to protect the area until he managed to get an agreement. But the British wanted out. Negotiations became more difficult. Bahrain decided not to join the proposed country. Qatar followed about two weeks later. But our leaders kept working. On December 2, 1971 the federation of the United Arab Emirates was announced. Sheikh Zayed bin Sultan Al Nahyan was elected president of the new nation.

In the early days, Abu Dhabi's main obstacle to development had been a lack of human resources. In fact, until very recently, we have always had to cope with a shortage of trained and educated local people. In 1971, the problem was critical. We needed skilled UAE nationals to take on jobs in the government.

Beyond filling the senior posts, we had to establish ministries and departments in all seven emirates. Fortunately, there were qualified people from Dubai, Ras al Khaimah, Sharjah, and the northern emirates who were educated to step into some roles immediately. They had schools long before we did in Abu Dhabi and were therefore more likely to have received a basic education. The federal government drew heavily on this source of qualified, educated nationals. Nevertheless, we were still forced to import additional personnel to help run government departments, ministries, and educational facilities.

Tribal roots

When the nation was formed in 1971, the people here were not used to dealing with public institutions or large organizations. When they had a problem or a special need, they simply went to their tribal leader for help. Getting the local people to trust the government to take care of them, to look upon the president as head of the new country, and to see themselves as citizens of the United Arab Emirates was difficult. It meant changing an entire way of life and thinking which had been passed down from one generation to the next for hundreds of years.

Getting the loyalty of the nomadic desert tribes was especially difficult. They moved from place to place with the seasons. Their children never went to school. The elders simply passed on what they knew to the next generation. They were trained to be on the alert at all times because of the tribal conflicts that were so much a part of their lives. They worshiped, defended their land, and took care of their goats and camels. They were devoted to God, their tribe, and their tribal chief. There were no ministries, no departments, and no government. There was no sense of belonging to a wider community other than the tribal group.

Federation brought with it a different social structure. The tribal society gave people immediate access to their leader. Now the leader seemed far removed. Everything was different, unknown and, probably for many of them, a little frightening. They disliked the barriers now separating them from the leaders. Before they would accept the new situation, they needed proof that the central government would work for them. The new government had to show the locals that it was worthy of the people's trust.

Benefits

Involving the tribal chiefs was crucial to the new government. Some were appointed to the Federal Council or given important positions in the ministries. They gained knowledge about the new system which they passed on to the members of their tribes. But the most convincing arguments for the new government were the benefits to the people. These were in the form of assistance, education, electrical power, and continuing development.

Shortly after federation, the local government saw a need to evaluate the land grant program. Many locals had benefited from the government gift of land. Others, however, were uninterested in doing anything with the land. Land development took time and effort, and they had no idea where to begin. Rather than building on the land, they sold their land at low prices. They usually got only 10,000 dirhams.

This was excellent value for the buyers. The sellers, however, used the cash immediately. Once the cash ran out they were right back to where they had started. This prompted the government to establish a ruling whereby those who had been given land were allowed to rent it to expatriates who could then build on it for commercial purposes.

Winning over the world

In addition to overseeing the affairs of our new country, Sheikh Zayed also focused on foreign relations. One goal Sheikh Zayed set was to get world recognition of the UAE as an independent country. It was a big task. To most people outside the Gulf region, we were an unknown people with a mysterious culture and a nomadic way of life. Even our Arab neighbors to the north were unfamiliar with us before we became a country in 1971.

The acceptance we desired was not easy to get. It took many years before we were accepted by most major countries. This was much longer than other new countries.

Sheikh Zayed tried as much as possible to maintain good relationships with our Arab brothers throughout the region. In one case, with the Saudis, he managed to repair a relationship torn by land disputes. In 1974 an agreement was signed.   One hundred and seventy years of struggle was over. Immediately thereafter Saudi Arabia recognized the United Arab Emirates.

Our ruler knew that as a young country we must maintain good relationships. We had to get along with other Arab nations. We had to get along with our Muslim brothers worldwide. We also had to get along with our international trading partners.   It was, and still is, important that we contribute as a member of the international community.

Chapter 8 - **Shifting Sands**

Money problems

Having lived simply for so many years, Abu Dhabians were unable to cope with the amount of change we were experiencing. The transition from poverty to sudden wealth was problematic. When they were given large sums of money, many local people had no idea what to do with it. They had to do something, either invest it or spend it. Since most knew nothing about investing, many went out and bought big ticket items for which they had little need.

This is exactly what happened when Sheikh Zayed decided to pay Abu Dhabians compensation for property which had been taken for town planning purposes between 1966 and 1968. People had received a large sum when their land was first turned over to the government. Ten years later, however, Sheikh Zayed felt they needed more money to help get them on their feet again. As part of the second compensation program of 1979 and 1980, many local inhabitants were paid hundreds of thousands, even millions, of dirhams. Most of the money was well spent. But, just as had happened with the first compensation program, some people were soon parted from their money either through bad luck or poor investments.

Someone I knew decided to go into the taxi business with the money he had been awarded through the second compensation program. He bought ten Toyota saloon cars to start his fleet and hired an equal number of drivers without knowing much more than their names. Before he knew it the drivers had all ran away with the brand new cars!

Inexperience in handling money was everyone's downfall. Local government rules were put in place to protect us as we learned to make financial decisions. For example, the UAE Central Bank passed a ruling limiting the amount banks could lend for personal loans. In addition, throughout the 1970s and 1980s, banks had accepted land, homes, and commercial buildings as collateral against loans. When local businessmen failed in business and couldn't repay their loans, the banks often took their homes and property. This meant that some Abu Dhabians found themselves in the street with nothing. Now the banks are much more cautious about whom they lend money to and for what reason. At the same time, those who could lose everything if their business fails will at least have a house to live in. Both the banks and the businessmen learned valuable lessons.

War

In 1982 war broke out between Iran and Iraq. While this negatively affected business in other Gulf countries, it was a boon to the UAE. Being distant from the center of combat, we were viewed as a neutral country by the warring countries, both of whom relied on our strategic position for the supply of basic needs such as food. The ports of the UAE were big enough to handle the volume of goods they required. So, instead of receiving goods in their own respective ports, both Iran and Iraq depended on ours. Most of the goods were offloaded in Dubai or Jebel Ali and then transported either in small boats across the Gulf to Iran or overland by truck to Iraq in the north. The war benefited our economy by increasing the amount of goods passing through our ports and boosting the demand for various products supplied by local traders. In addition, many oil companies operating in Iran moved to the UAE. They continued to supply them, from here, with fast moving consumer goods and basic needs.

Surprisingly, tourism also increased in the Emirates during that period. Tourism was a welcome industry in Abu Dhabi. It helped diversify and strengthen an economy which was, and still is, so dependent on the oil industry. Tourism also gave us the opportunity to show the outside world how much we had achieved in the few short years since development had begun. The UAE has a lot to offer visitors: history, a unique culture, a warm winter climate, fabulous desert scenery, crystal clear waters, rugged mountains, and modern cities.

While the Iran-Iraq war and the growing tourist trade contributed to our growth, the expansion of the oil industry in Abu Dhabi was also at its height in the 1980s. The oil companies tried wherever possible to involve local merchants and businessmen.

This mutually beneficial relationship between the oil companies and the local business community remains strong today. It is one of the pillars of our successful economy and, I believe, unique.

Chapter 9 - **Persistence Pays Off**

Beyond our Dreams

My family completed the Corniche Hotel in Abu Dhabi in 1982. We immediately began to look for a place to build a similar hotel in Dubai. We bought a piece of land on the Al Maktoum Road. As soon as word got out that we had purchased the lot to build a hotel, the value of the land next to it rose rapidly. We found ourselves in a position where it was far better to sell the new land at a big profit rather than go ahead with our building plans. We looked at several other sites, but whenever we bought, we found ourselves in a similar situation. We were making money in the real estate business instead of the hotel trade.

Finally, in 1988 we purchased a small plot of land close to the Trade Centre on the Abu Dhabi - Dubai road. I felt it would be an excellent location for a hotel. Unfortunately, we found out later that the plot we had purchased was too small for the size of the hotel that we wanted to build. In addition, I had begun to think of a project involving more than just a hotel. I would need more land for the larger scale development project I had in mind. I approached my father. He was very receptive. Together we wrote a letter to Sheikh Maktoum, the Ruler of Dubai, outlining the project. Sheikh Maktoum was more than generous in response. He gave us a plot of land twice the size of the one we already had at no cost. The land was a generous gift from Sheikh Maktoum. Our project had a hotel, an office complex, an apartment building, and a shopping center.

The project took about five years to complete. We started in 1989 and finished in 1994. During that time, Iraq invaded Kuwait causing a war which, it was feared, might spill over into neighbouring countries. Because of that, people transferred their savings out of the country. Many foreigners shut down their shops or businesses and left. Like most of my friends, I stayed, continued to work, and saw the war through to its end.

Thanks to Sheikh Zayed's wisdom we had managed to avoid any regional conflicts until Saddam Hussein invaded Kuwait. When that happened, we could no longer remain neutral as the UAE was on Saddam's list of possible targets. We gave our wholehearted support to the Kuwaitis. We all thank God the war was short and ended in favor of the Kuwaitis.

Despite the war, the hotel was finally finished. At a time when everyone was very unsure of what the future held, we continued. The Dubai Holiday Centre, which cost 465 million dirhams to build, was opened in the summer of 1994 and fully finished by the end of the same year. It hosted a major conference shortly afterwards and continues to do very well. Immediately upon its completion, we received an offer of 1.2 billion dirhams for the property. We rejected it despite the fact that the offer was almost three times what it had cost to build.

The Dubai property is more than just another business holding for our Group. To us it is a symbol. It is evidence of what a local businessman can do, given the opportunity and the support. It is the culmination of five years of intense efforts during a period of war and uncertainty. It is proof of our belief that investing money into our own economy is more worthwhile than investing it in the banks of Europe and America.

The Dubai Holiday Centre is an outstanding example of the generosity of our Rulers, especially Sheikh Maktoum. The Dubai Government's support during the project made our job easier. The local government connected us to all the services from electricity to sewage without extra costs or delays. Today, we have a deluxe 650-room property serving not only the residents of Dubai, but the whole region.

It is gratifying to see this achievement. More so because it is the result of hard work, dedication and a belief in our ability to do something important, to make a contribution to the growth of our economy and to the well-being of all who live in the Emirates. I believe every citizen in the UAE must participate in the development of our country, especially since we, the people of the Emirates, are so few in number. We are the minority in our own country.

Nevertheless, we should be able to provide for the majority. In fact, it is our responsibility to do so. We are the hosts of all others who work in our country, helping us to move forward, develop, and expand our economy. We have a responsibility to those people and to ourselves. We must believe in the UAE. It is our duty to maximize the use of all our resources, work together to realize the vision of our leaders, and make this country an example for others to follow.

Faith, hope and perseverance

The Dubai Holiday Centre is but one of hundreds of success stories to be found in the United Arab Emirates. Our achievements over the past thirty years, both as individuals and as a nation, are astounding. The transformation resulting from our efforts has taken us from rags to riches in less than a generation.

The small fishing settlement which counted less than fifteen hundred people in 1950 is now a modern city with a population of over a million people. We live in modern housing and high rise buildings instead of huts made of palm fronds or mud. We have air conditioning to cool us in the heat of summer and blankets, jackets, and sweaters to warm ourselves during the chill winter evenings. We no longer drink brackish water drawn from hand-dug wells and hauled to our homes in goat skins. We have fresh desalinated water piped directly wherever we need it. We no longer wash in the sea. Instead we shower and bathe in the comfort of marbled and mirrored bathrooms.

We have modern hospitals to care for the sick. Children, who might have been orphaned thirty years ago, now grow up with their mother's love. We do not travel by camel anymore. Now we drive in high-powered motorcars. What was once a seven-day journey from Abu Dhabi to Al Ain now takes less than two hours. The rough tracks that wound between our barasti huts and across the sand have been replaced by a well-planned road system. Our children are educated at private schools, both here and abroad. Gone are the days of the ill-equipped schoolhouse with a single teacher.

Our generation, and the one which preceded it, have laid the foundation for a bright future. However, as everyone knows, the only sure thing about tomorrow is that, God willing, the sun will continue to rise in the east and set in the west. Beyond that, the future is in no way certain. Our children and our children's children will have to work hard. They must conserve what we have created and ensure that our rags-to-riches story is told to future generations, so they too understand the value of faith, hope, and perseverance.

Education is the key

Of the many lessons we learned, two tower above all the others in importance. First and foremost is to have faith in God. Without Him we are nothing. The second lesson is that education is one of the most powerful tools of a growing nation. Without education, a society can fall apart and die. The little amount of education my generation and I received was not enough, even for our time and place. Our children and their children will have more opportunities to pursue higher levels of education. I only hope they do not let those opportunities pass them by. I encourage them to reach out and grab every chance they get to equip themselves with the tools that only good schooling can give.

I have written this book in hope - hope that the efforts of my generation and the generations before us will not be in vain. Hope that our children will take courage from our stories as they work at making the future even better. I hope that our educational efforts will help the next generation to do better than we have done.

I also hope that our federation will survive well into the future, united and strong. For almost forty years, we lived under the protection of a wise and thoughtful leader, Sheikh Zayed bin Sultan Al Nahyan. We must maintain the unity he worked for so long to achieve. We must take pride in our accomplishments. Finally, we must face any threat to the strength of our country. It is fundamental to our very survival and the security of future generations.

Glossary

abbaya	cloak
agal	headcloth-cord
anna	16 to the rupee
barasti	huts made of palm tree wood
dhub	lizard
dishdash	long, sleeved shirt- like man's garment
gutra	headcloth
kandoura	(as "dishdash")
majlis	a room for receiving guests
mulla	religious teacher
rupee	Indian coin
sabkha	salt-flat
shamal	strong wind from North
souk	bazaar